# MY FRIEND EMBARRASSED ME

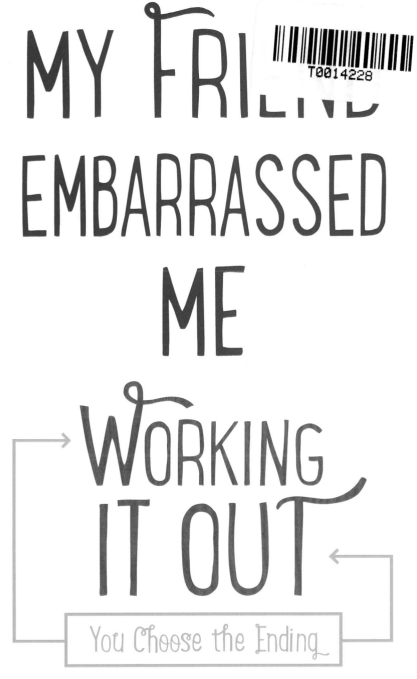

## WORKING IT OUT

You Choose the Ending

by Connie Colwell Miller • illustrated by Sofia Cardoso

Do you ever wish you could change a story or choose a different ending?

**IN THESE BOOKS, YOU CAN!**

Read along and when you see this:

## WHAT HAPPENS NEXT?

→ Skip to the page for that choice, and see what happens.

In this story, Abdi's friend Cora embarrasses him. Will Abdi work things out with his friend, or will he lash back? YOU make the choices!

At recess, Abdi and his best friend Cora choose teams for a game of baseball. When it's Abdi's turn, he chooses Rylie. "I knew you'd pick Rylie!" Cora blurts. "You have such a crush on her!"

TURN THE PAGE →

Everyone turns to look at Abdi, including Rylie. Some kids giggle. Abdi's cheeks burn with embarrassment. "Oh, gosh, Abdi," she whispers to him. "I'm sorry. It just slipped out."

WHAT HAPPENS NEXT?

If Abdi yells at Cora, turn the page.
If Abdi stays calm, turn to page 12.

"Well, YOU have a crush on Adam!" Abdi shouts. He knows he shouldn't share Cora's secret, but he is angry. He is glad kids are looking at Cora and not him.

## WHAT HAPPENS NEXT?

→ If Abdi keeps teasing Cora, turn the page.

If Abdi takes Cora aside to talk, turn to page 16. ←

"In fact, since you like Adam so much, why don't you marry him," Abdi taunts. More kids laugh.
Tears well up in Cora's eyes.

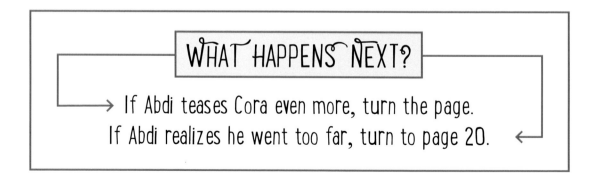

## WHAT HAPPENS NEXT?

→ If Abdi teases Cora even more, turn the page.
If Abdi realizes he went too far, turn to page 20.

TURN THE PAGE →

"I said I was sorry, Abdi," Cora says.

Abdi doesn't stop. "Cora and Adam sitting in a tree . . ." he sings.

Cora bursts into tears and runs off the field. Abdi realizes that lashing back at Cora made the situation worse. Now he will have to play baseball without his friend.

THE END

Go to page 23.

Abdi is embarrassed and a little angry. But he can tell Cora didn't mean to hurt him.

"I really am sorry, Abdi," Cora says.

"I just need a minute," Abdi says. He goes to the bench and reties his shoes. He looks for Rylie. She is warming up with another friend and seems to have already forgotten what happened.

TURN THE PAGE →

After a few minutes, Abdi rejoins his friends. The kids play a fun game of baseball, and Abdi is glad he didn't make a fuss. Everyone forgot about his embarrassment and played the game.

THE END

→ Go to page 23. ←

"Look, Cora. I'm sorry for what I said. But you embarrassed me."

"I know," Cora says. "I'm sorry, too."

TURN THE PAGE →

"Do you still want to play the game?" Cora asks.

Abdi remembers something his father told him. His dad said that people forget other people's embarrassing moments quickly.

"Yes, let's play," Abdi says. He returns to the field with Cora, and they start their game.

THE END

→ Go to page 23. ←

Abdi looks at his friend's face and realizes he's gone too far. "Cora, can we talk over here?" he asks.

TURN THE PAGE →

"I'm sorry for what I said," Abdi admits. "You embarrassed me, and I got mad. I think maybe we need some time to cool off." Abdi and Cora both leave the game. They spend some time apart.

THE END

## THINK AGAIN

- What happened at the end of the path you chose?
- Did you like that ending?
- Go back to page 3. Read the story again and pick different choices. How did the story change?

We all can choose how to act when we are embarrassed. If your friend embarrassed you, would YOU lash back, or would you try to work it out?

AMICUS ILLUSTRATED is published by Amicus
P.O. Box 227, Mankato, MN 56002
www.amicuspublishing.us

Library of Congress Cataloging-in-Publication Data
Names: Miller, Connie Colwell, 1976- author. | Cardoso, Sofia
   (Illustrator), illustrator.
Title: My friend embarrassed me : working it out : you choose the ending /
   by Connie Colwell Miller ; illustrated by Sofia Cardoso.
Description: Mankato, MN : Amicus. [2023] | Series: Making good choices |
   Audience: Ages 6-9 | Audience: Grades 2-3 | Summary: "In this choose-your-
own-ending picture book, Cora lets slip that Abdi has a crush on Riley. Abdi is
embarrassed. Will he retaliate or accept Cora's apology? Readers make choices
for Abdi, with each story path leading to different outcomes. Includes four
endings and discussion questions."—Provided by publisher.
Identifiers: LCCN 2021056681 (print) | LCCN 2021056682 (ebook) | ISBN
   9781645492788 (hardcover) | ISBN 9781681528021 (paperback) | ISBN
   9781645493662 (ebook)
Subjects: LCSH: Embarrassment in children--Juvenile literature. |
   Friendship in children--Juvenile literature.
Classification: LCC BF723.E44 .M55 2023 (print) | LCC BF723.E44 (ebook) |
   DDC 152.4--dc23/eng/20211217
LC record available at https://lccn.loc.gov/2021056681
LC ebook record available at https://lccn.loc.gov/2021056682

Editor: Rebecca Glaser
Series Designer: Kathleen Petelinsek
Book Designer: Catherine Berthiaume

## ABOUT THE AUTHOR

Connie Colwell Miller is a writer, editor, and instructor who lives in Le Sueur, Minnesota, with her four children. She has written over 100 books for young children. She likes to tell stories to her kids to teach them important life lessons.

## ABOUT THE ILLUSTRATOR

Sofia Cardoso is a Portuguese children's book illustrator, designer, and foodie, whose passion for illustration goes all the way back to her childhood years. Using a mix of both traditional and digital methods, she now spends her days creating whimsical illustrations, full of color and young characters that aim to inspire joy and creativity in both kids and kids at heart.